MY SPIDER STUDY JOURNAL

This journal
belongs to

____

____

____

Contents

How to use this journal?

Spiders are not insects, in case you didn't know. They are a form of animal known as an "arachnid." Arachnology is the scientific study of spiders and other related species. Arachnologists research spiders and their venom by paying close attention to and documenting information such as anatomical structure, habitat, appearance, eating habits, and reproduction.

The "Spider anatomy" page includes a diagram as well as the anatomical terms used to describe the body parts of a spider.

The "log pages" consist of one plain sheet followed by a ruled sheet. On the plain sheet, draw or paste pictures of the spider and mention the name. The details can be documented on the ruled page.

On the "Did you Know?" page at the end of this journal, you will find a list of interesting facts about spiders from around the world.

The final page is provided for making a phone number list. You should write down the phone numbers of a few doctors in your area (in case of a spider bite), nature/science society in your area, and possibly the phone numbers of friends who are interested in spiders.

Spiders can be studied at home and in the backyard. However, adult supervision is necessary if children are present.

Spider Anatomy

The main body of a spider is divided into two parts.
1. Cephalothorax: The head and thorax fused together
2. Opisthosoma: The abdomen

Typically, spiders have eight legs that are used for walking. Each leg is divided into seven sections. Starting from the body, they are the coxa, trochanter, femur, patella, tibia, metatarsus, and tarsus. Claws differing in number and size, adorn the tip of tarsus. Webspinners have three claws and hunting spiders have two claws. Some spiders do not have claws at all.

They also have a pair of appendages in front of the legs known as "pedipalps". They are used for touching, tasting, and handling prey.

The mouth part of a spider is called "chelicerae". The venom produced by the spiders is inserted into prey through the chelicerae fangs.

The abdomen is connected to the cephalothorax by a thin "pedicel". This allows the spider to move the abdomen without moving the cephalothorax while spinning webs.

The "spinnerets" are a movable, telescopic organ in the bottom of the abdomen that is used for silk spinning. Depending on the species, they are arranged in one to four pairs. They produce spider silk, which is used to make a sticky web that traps other insects.

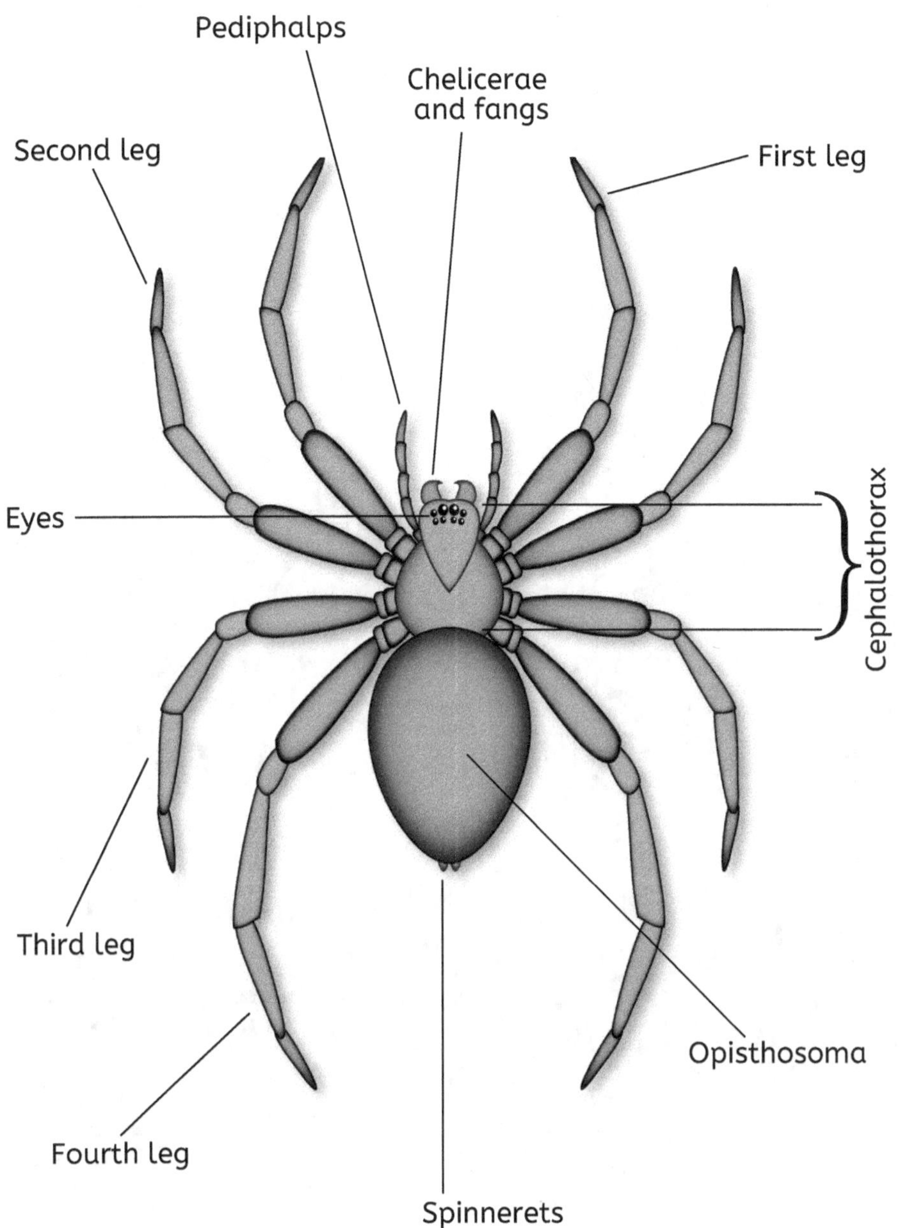

Pediphalps
Chelicerae
and fangs
Second leg
First leg
Eyes
Cephalothorax
Third leg
Opisthosoma
Fourth leg
Spinnerets

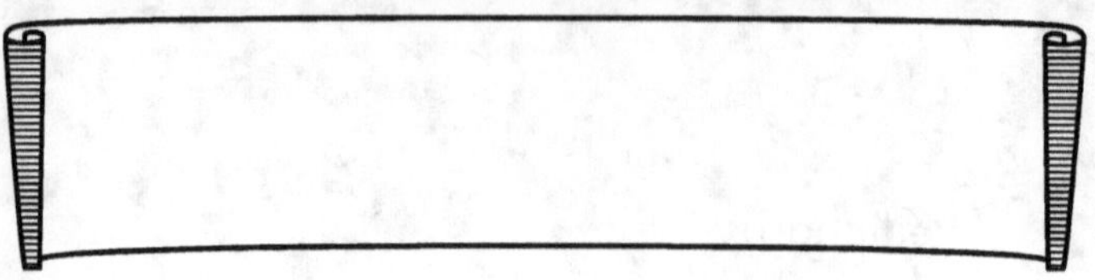

Scientific name:

Other local names:

Description:

Eating habits:

Habitat:

Web construction:

Other observations:

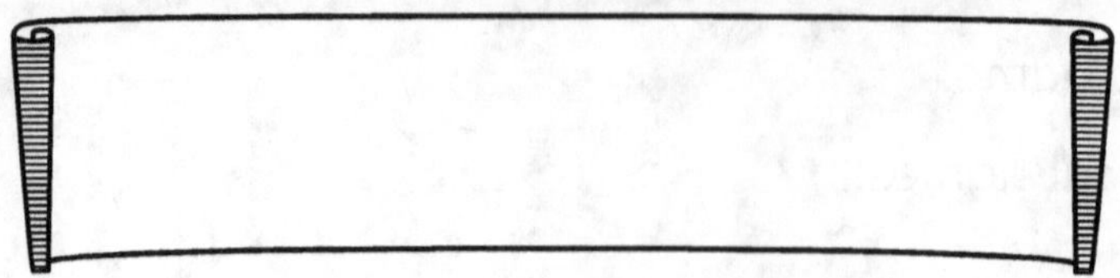

Scientific name:

Other local names:

Description:

Eating habits:

Habitat:

Web construction:

Other observations:

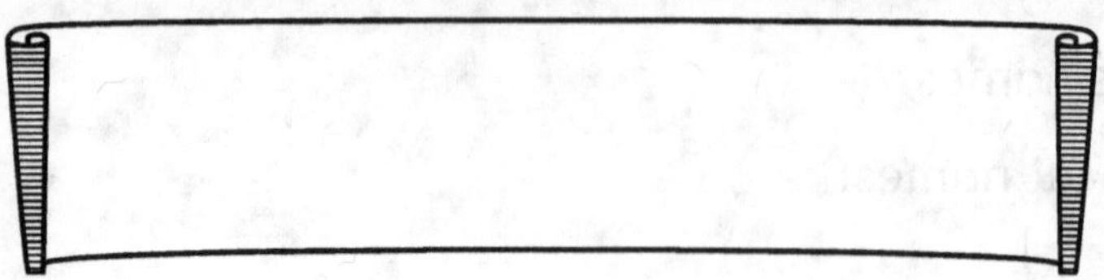

Scientific name:

Other local names:

Description:

Eating habits:

Habitat:

Web construction:

Other observations:

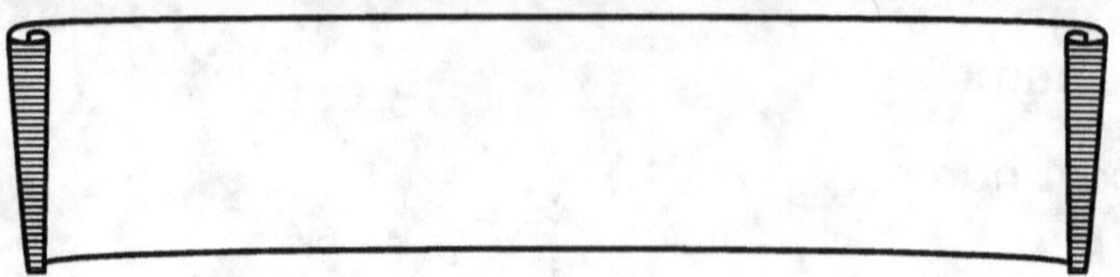

Scientific name:

Other local names:

Description:

Eating habits:

Habitat:

Web construction:

Other observations:

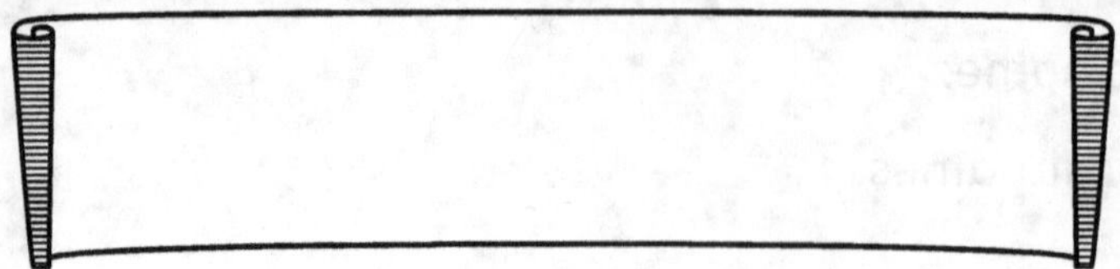

Scientific name:

Other local names:

Description:

Eating habits:

Habitat:

Web construction:

Other observations:

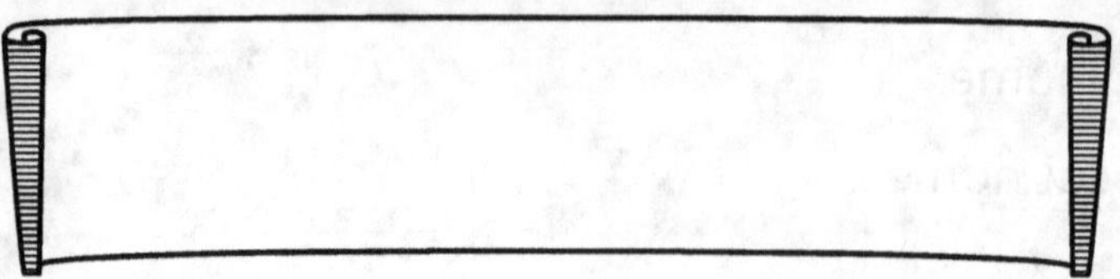

Scientific name:

Other local names:

Description:

Eating habits:

Habitat:

Web construction:

Other observations:

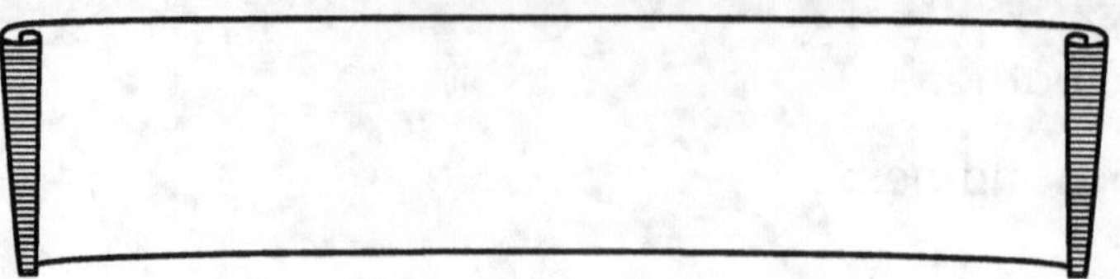

Scientific name:

Other local names:

Description:

Eating habits:

Habitat:

Web construction:

Other observations:

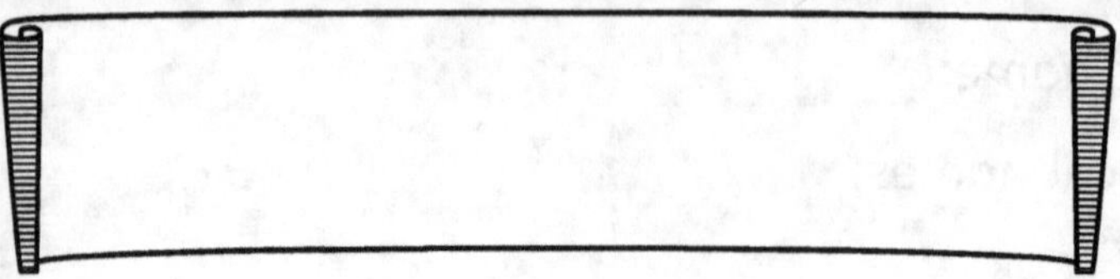

Scientific name:

Other local names:

Description:

Eating habits:

Habitat:

Web construction:

Other observations:

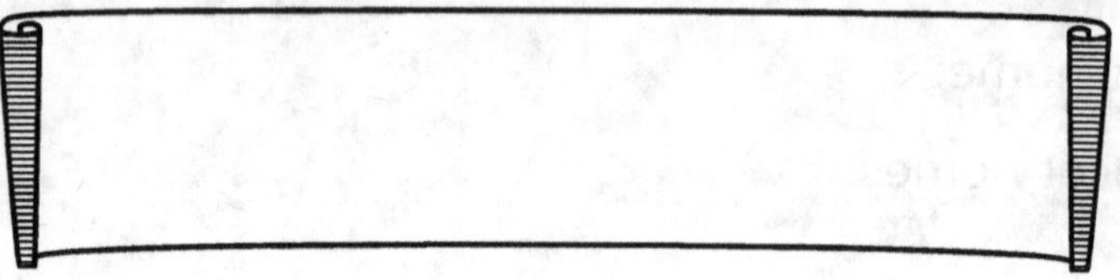

Scientific name:

Other local names:

Description:

Eating habits:

Habitat:

Web construction:

Other observations:

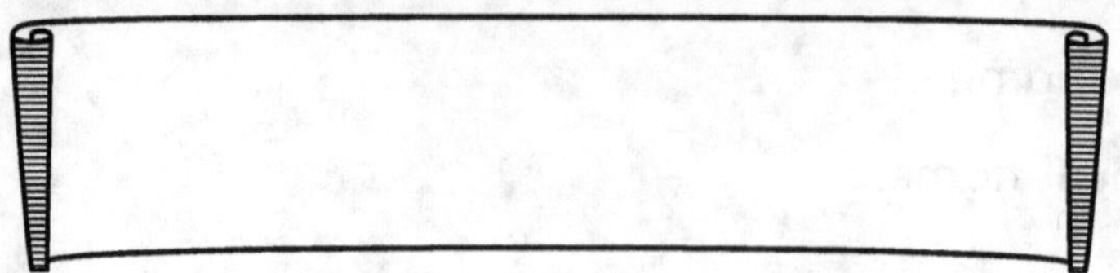

Scientific name:

Other local names:

Description:

Eating habits:

Habitat:

Web construction:

Other observations:

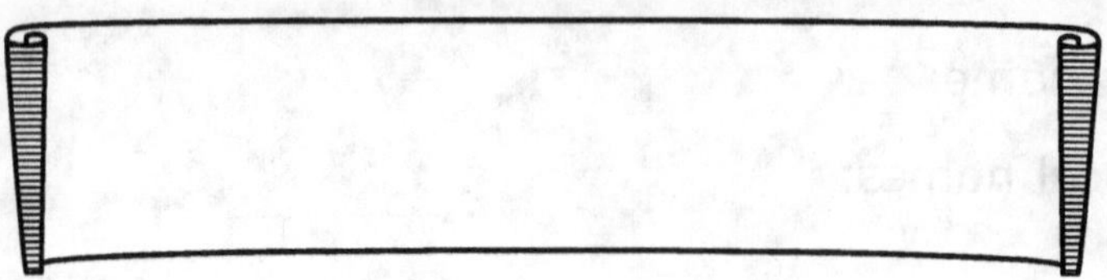

Scientific name:

Other local names:

Description:

Eating habits:

Habitat:

Web construction:

Other observations:

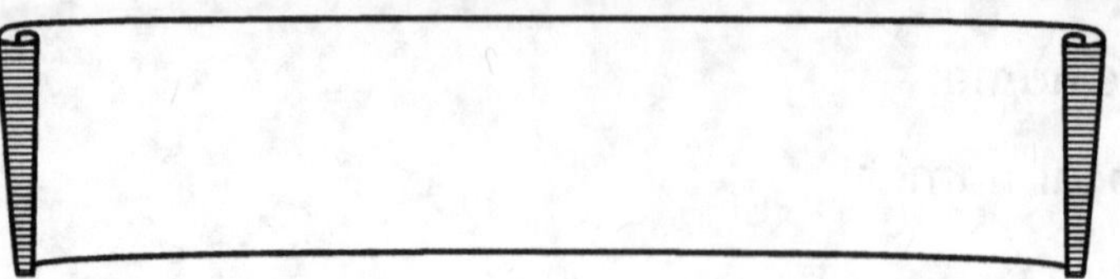

Scientific name:

Other local names:

Description:

Eating habits:

Habitat:

Web construction:

Other observations:

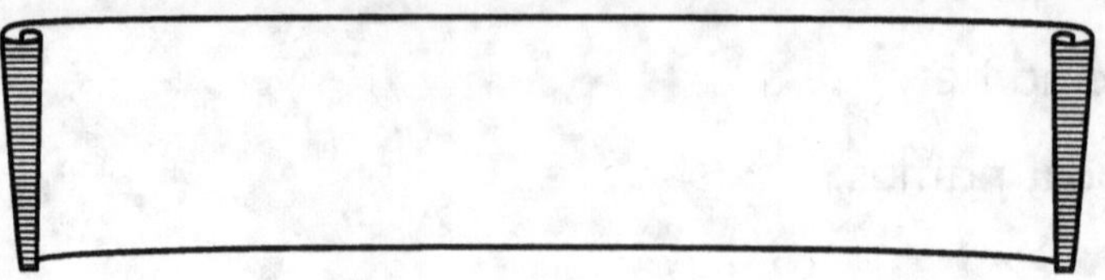

Scientific name:

Other local names:

Description:

Eating habits:

Habitat:

Web construction:

Other observations:

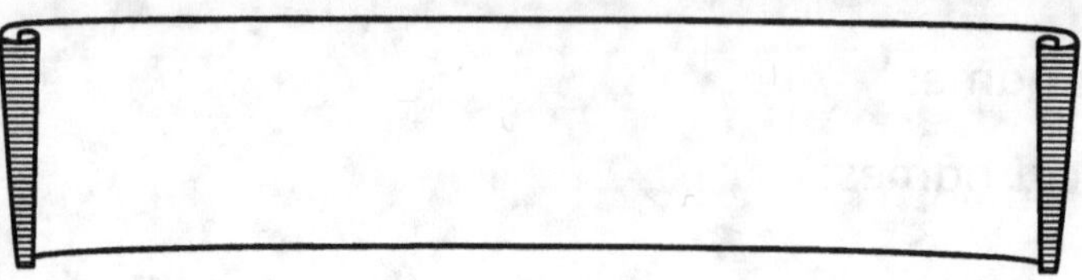

Scientific name:

Other local names:

Description:

Eating habits:

Habitat:

Web construction:

Other observations:

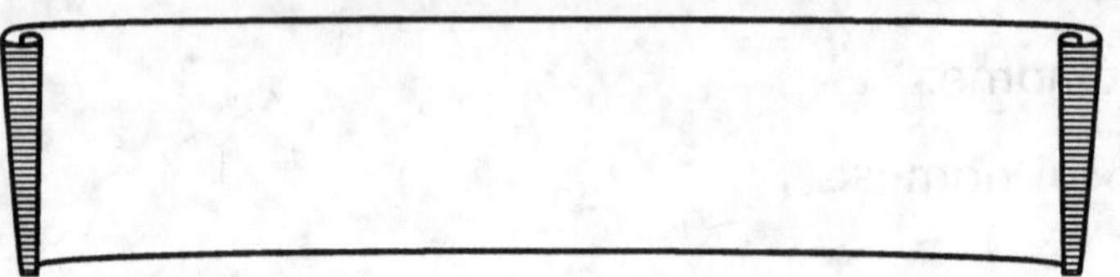

Scientific name:

Other local names:

Description:

Eating habits:

Habitat:

Web construction:

Other observations:

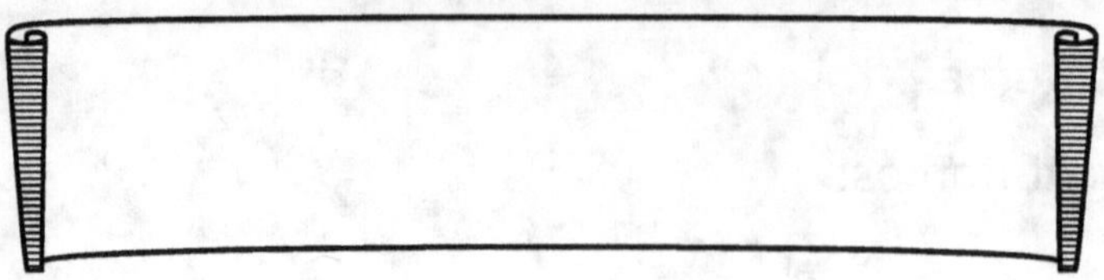

Scientific name:

Other local names:

Description:

Eating habits:

Habitat:

Web construction:

Other observations:

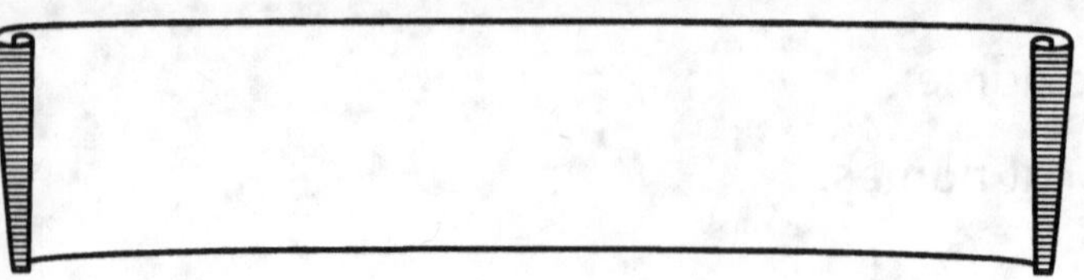

Scientific name:

Other local names:

Description:

Eating habits:

Habitat:

Web construction:

Other observations:

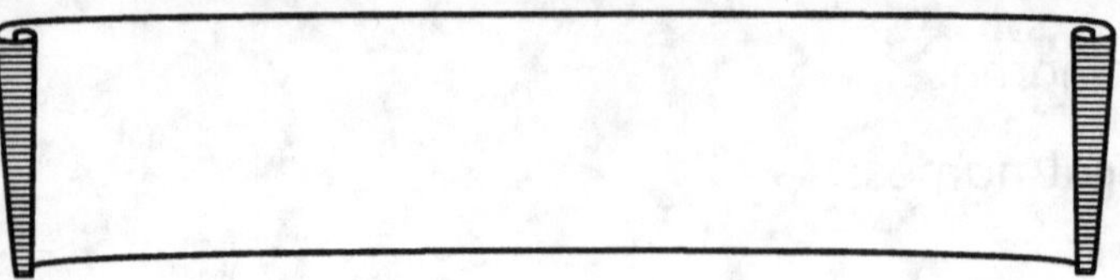

Scientific name:

Other local names:

Description:

Eating habits:

Habitat:

Web construction:

Other observations:

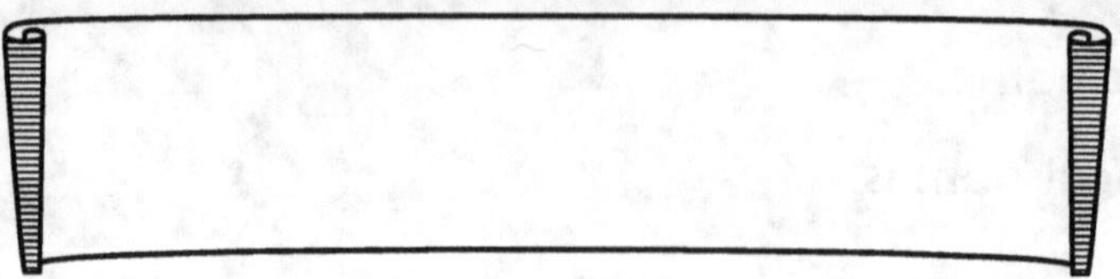

Scientific name:

Other local names:

Description:

Eating habits:

Habitat:

Web construction:

Other observations:

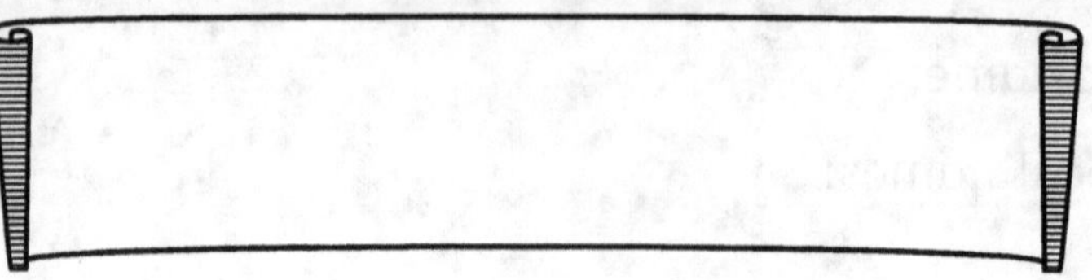

Scientific name:

Other local names:

Description:

Eating habits:

Habitat:

Web construction:

Other observations:

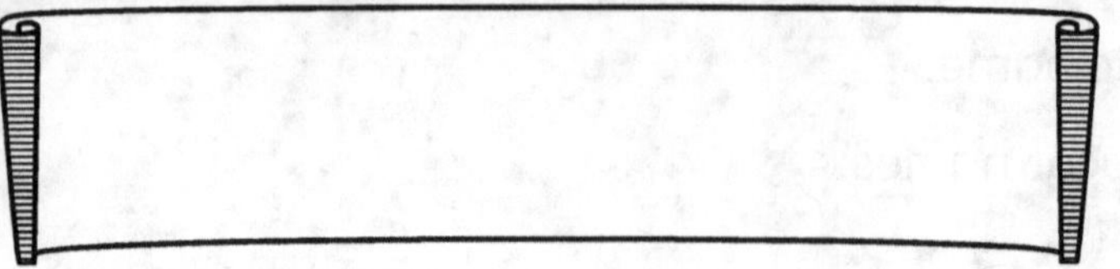

Scientific name:

Other local names:

Description:

Eating habits:

Habitat:

Web construction:

Other observations:

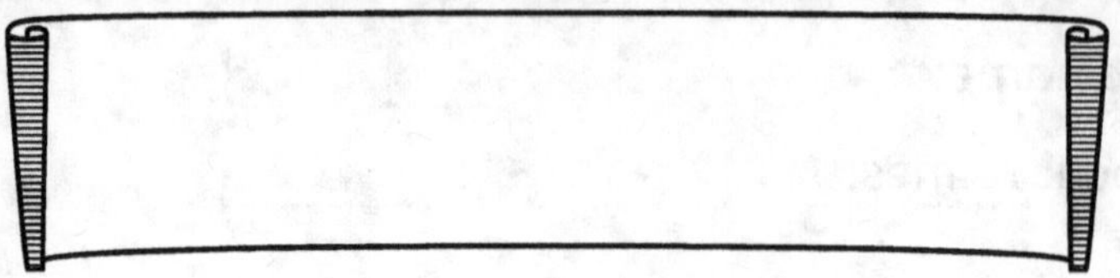

Scientific name:

Other local names:

Description:

Eating habits:

Habitat:

Web construction:

Other observations:

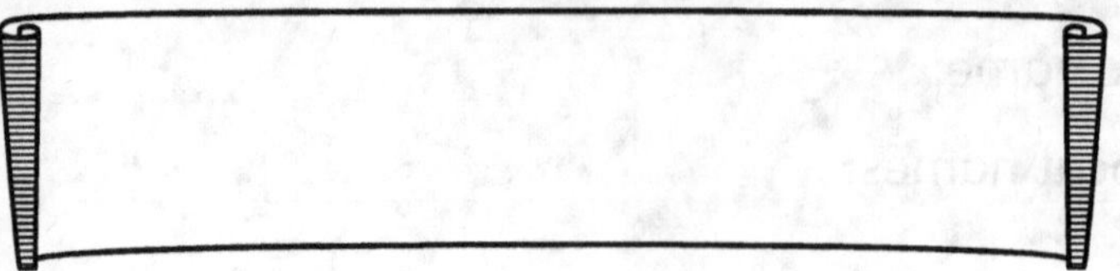

Scientific name:

Other local names:

Description:

Eating habits:

Habitat:

Web construction:

Other observations:

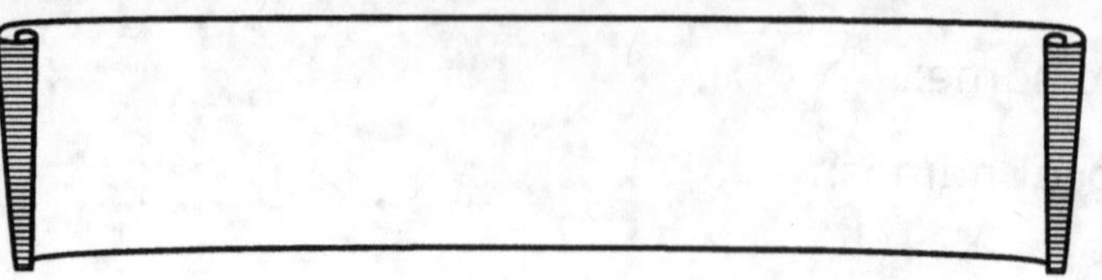

Scientific name:

Other local names:

Description:

Eating habits:

Habitat:

Web construction:

Other observations:

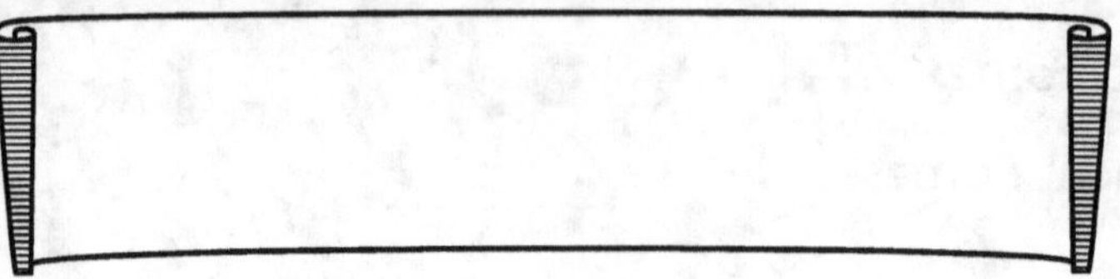

Scientific name:

Other local names:

Description:

Eating habits:

Habitat:

Web construction:

Other observations:

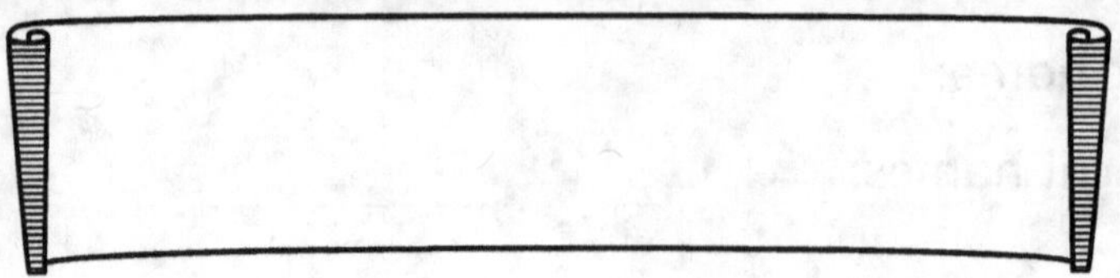

Scientific name:

Other local names:

Description:

Eating habits:

Habitat:

Web construction:

Other observations:

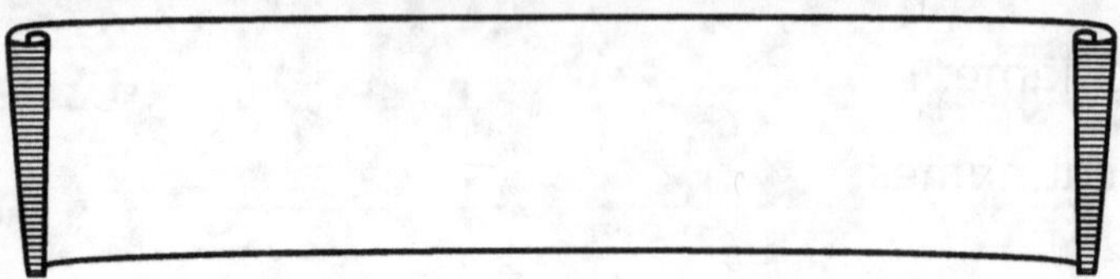

Scientific name:

Other local names:

Description:

Eating habits:

Habitat:

Web construction:

Other observations:

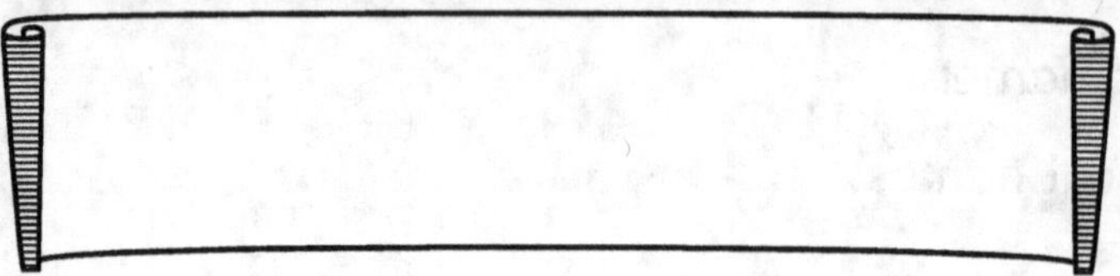

Scientific name:

Other local names:

Description:

Eating habits:

Habitat:

Web construction:

Other observations:

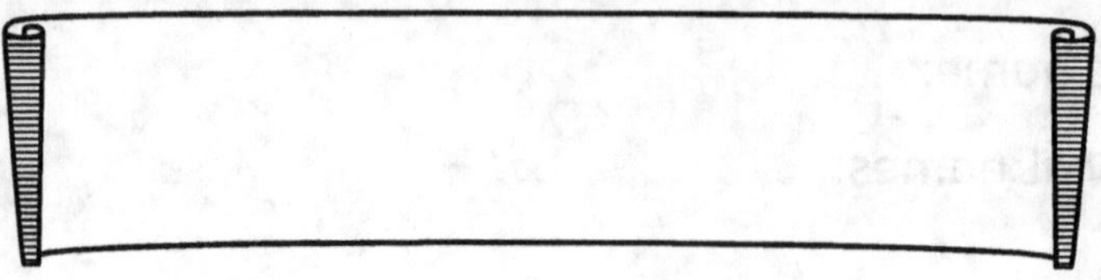

Scientific name:

Other local names:

Description:

Eating habits:

Habitat:

Web construction:

Other observations:

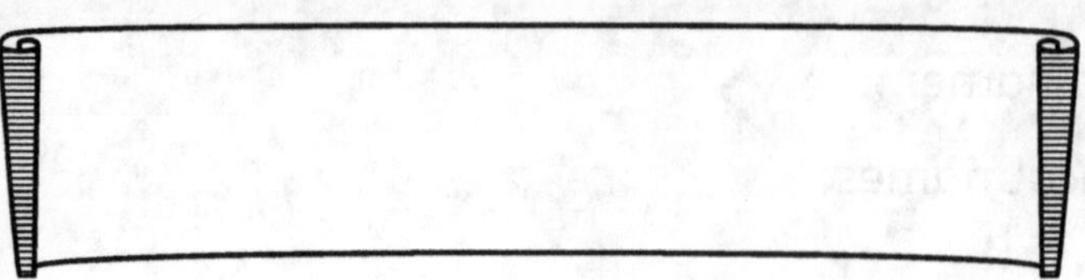

Scientific name:

Other local names:

Description:

Eating habits:

Habitat:

Web construction:

Other observations:

Scientific name:

Other local names:

Description:

Eating habits:

Habitat:

Web construction:

Other observations:

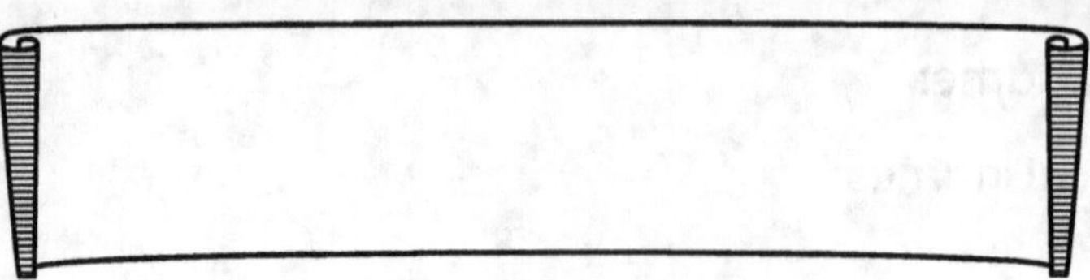

Scientific name:

Other local names:

Description:

Eating habits:

Habitat:

Web construction:

Other observations:

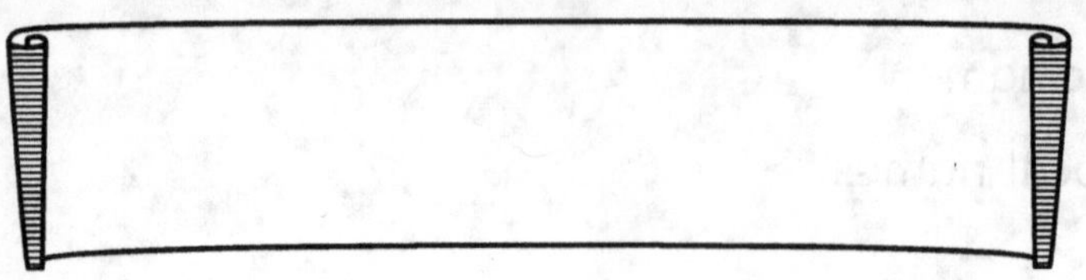

Scientific name:

Other local names:

Description:

Eating habits:

Habitat:

Web construction:

Other observations:

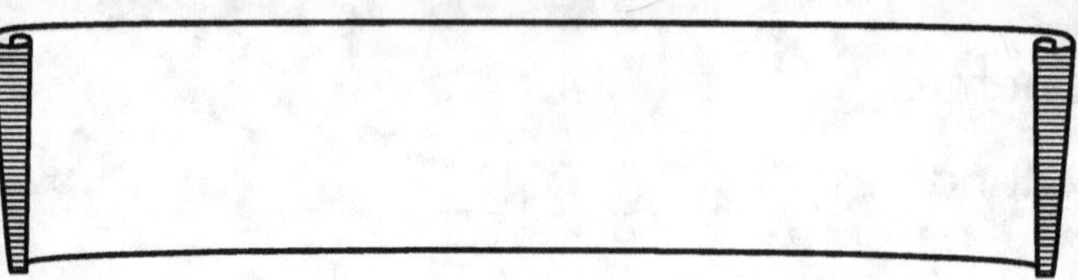

Scientific name:

Other local names:

Description:

Eating habits:

Habitat:

Web construction:

Other observations:

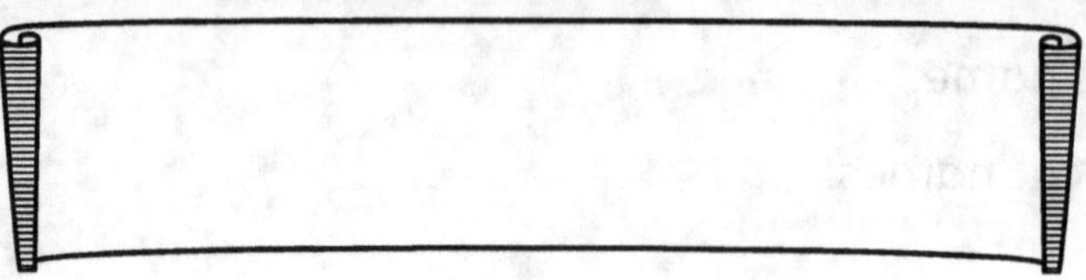

Scientific name:

Other local names:

Description:

Eating habits:

Habitat:

Web construction:

Other observations:

Scientific name:

Other local names:

Description:

Eating habits:

Habitat:

Web construction:

Other observations:

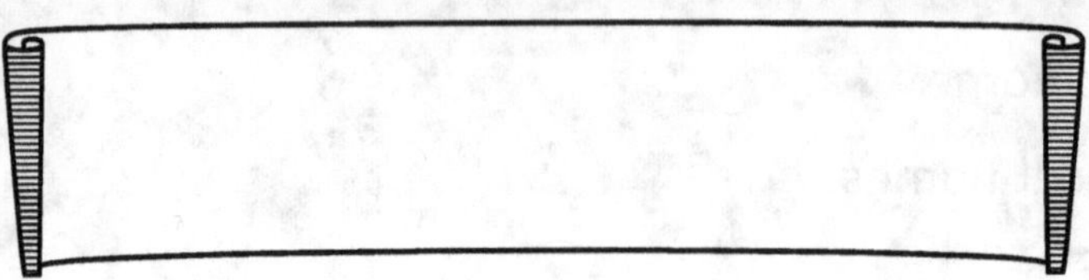

Scientific name:

Other local names:

Description:

Eating habits:

Habitat:

Web construction:

Other observations:

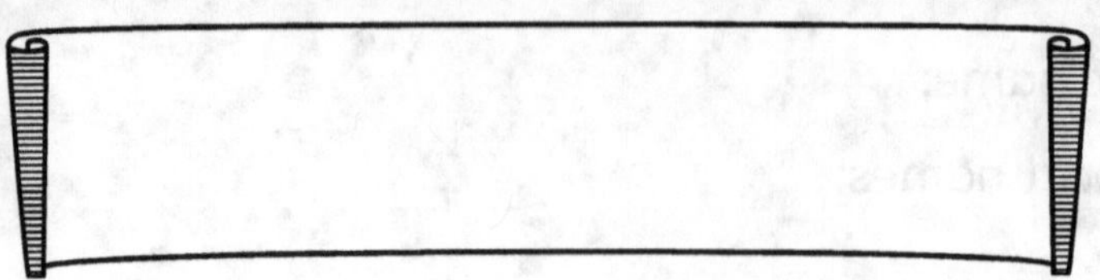

Scientific name:

Other local names:

Description:

Eating habits:

Habitat:

Web construction:

Other observations:

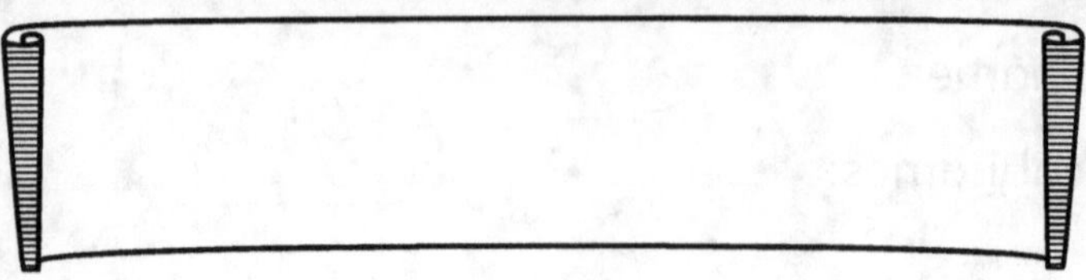

Scientific name:

Other local names:

Description:

Eating habits:

Habitat:

Web construction:

Other observations:

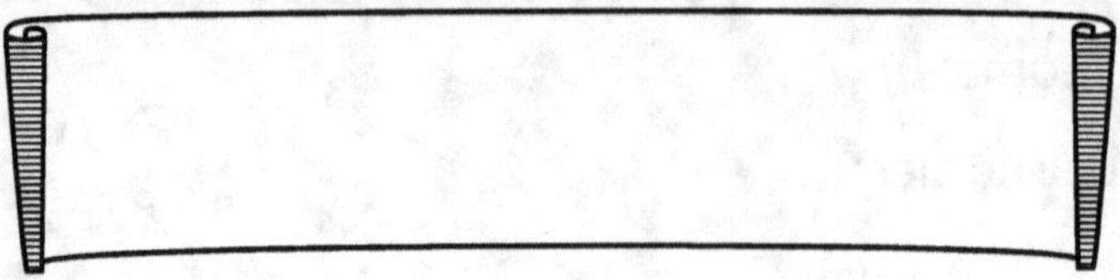

Scientific name:

Other local names:

Description:

Eating habits:

Habitat:

Web construction:

Other observations:

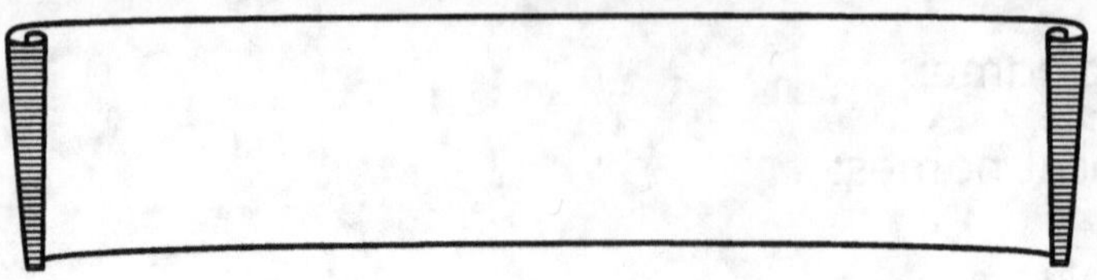

Scientific name:

Other local names:

Description:

Eating habits:

Habitat:

Web construction:

Other observations:

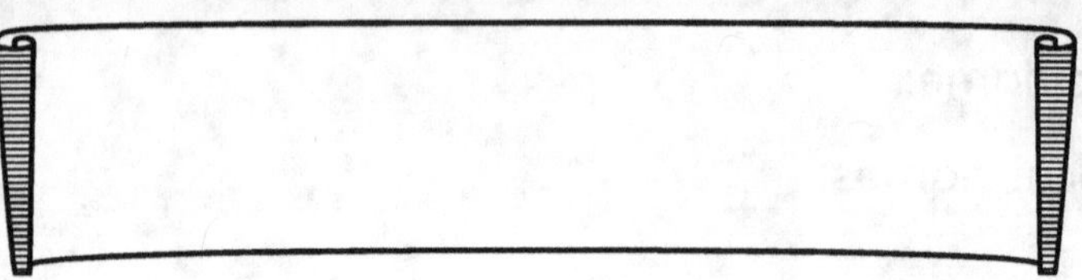

Scientific name:

Other local names:

Description:

Eating habits:

Habitat:

Web construction:

Other observations:

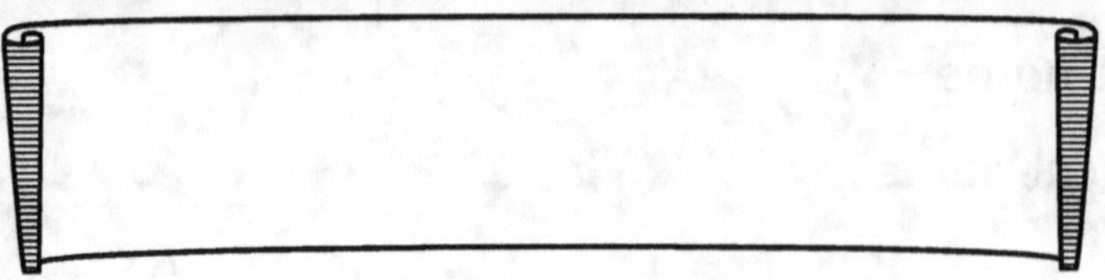

Scientific name:

Other local names:

Description:

Eating habits:

Habitat:

Web construction:

Other observations:

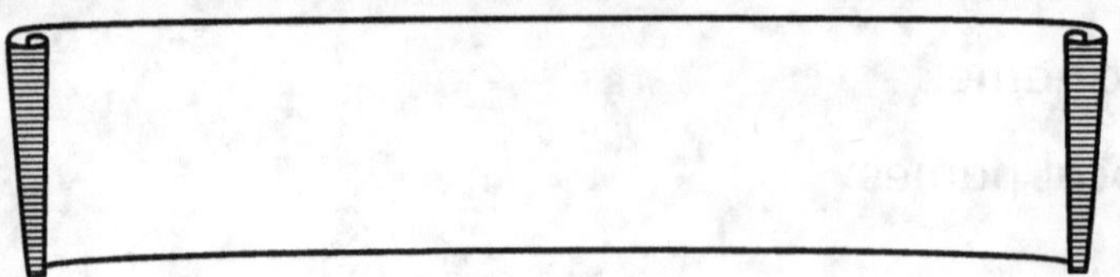

Scientific name:

Other local names:

Description:

Eating habits:

Habitat:

Web construction:

Other observations:

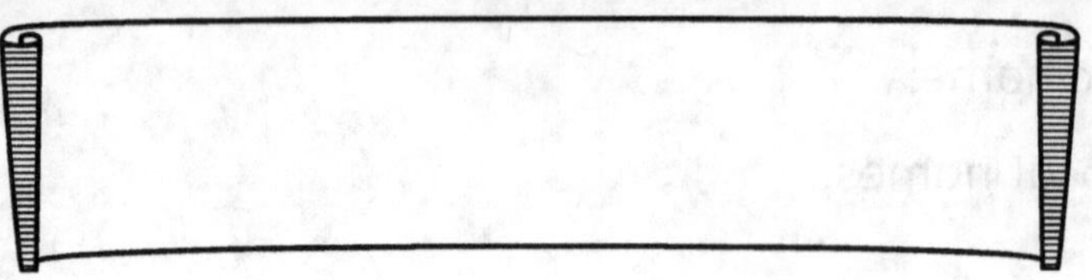

Scientific name:

Other local names:

Description:

Eating habits:

Habitat:

Web construction:

Other observations:

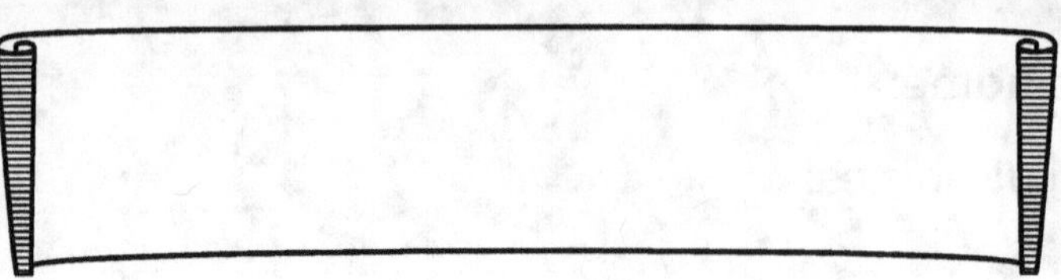

Scientific name:

Other local names:

Description:

Eating habits:

Habitat:

Web construction:

Other observations:

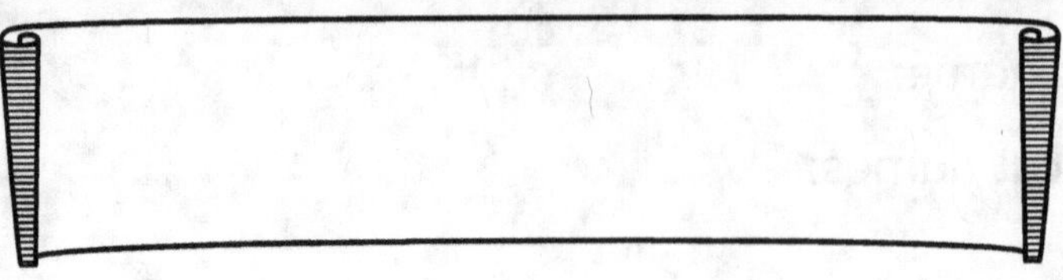

Scientific name:

Other local names:

Description:

Eating habits:

Habitat:

Web construction:

Other observations:

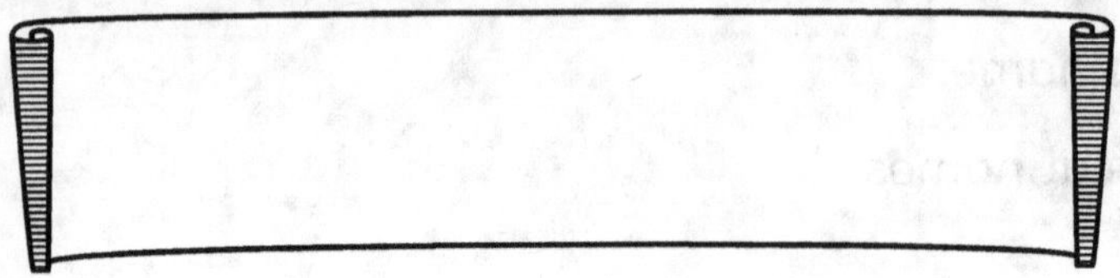

Scientific name:

Other local names:

Description:

Eating habits:

Habitat:

Web construction:

Other observations:

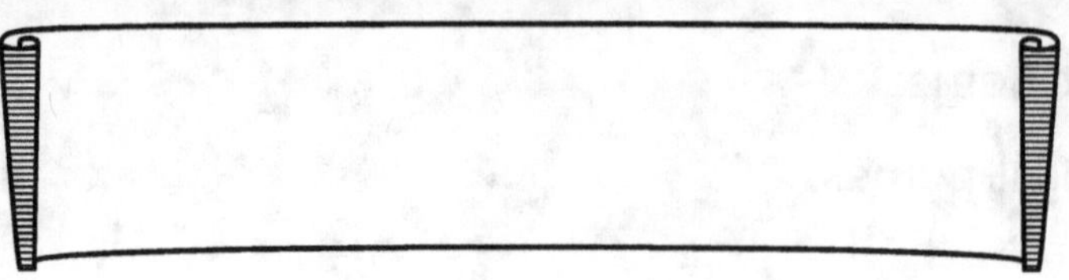

Scientific name:

Other local names:

Description:

Eating habits:

Habitat:

Web construction:

Other observations:

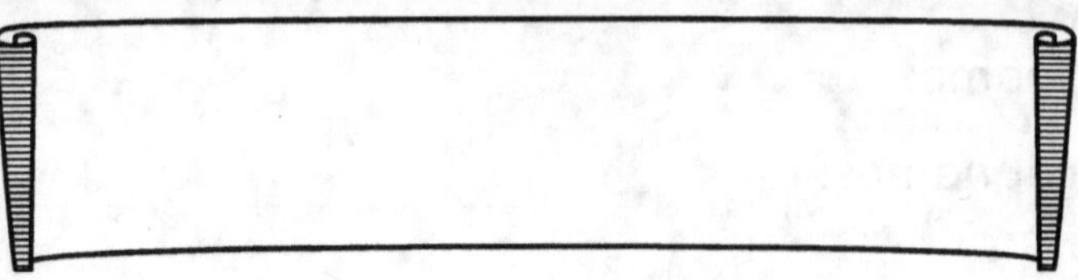

Scientific name:

Other local names:

Description:

Eating habits:

Habitat:

Web construction:

Other observations:

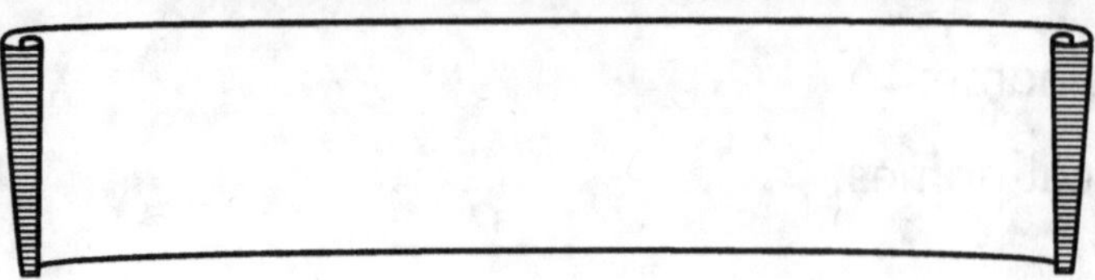

Scientific name:

Other local names:

Description:

Eating habits:

Habitat:

Web construction:

Other observations:

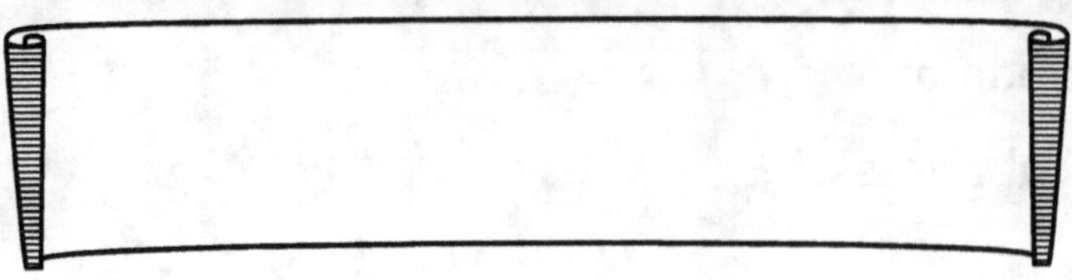

Scientific name:

Other local names:

Description:

Eating habits:

Habitat:

Web construction:

Other observations:

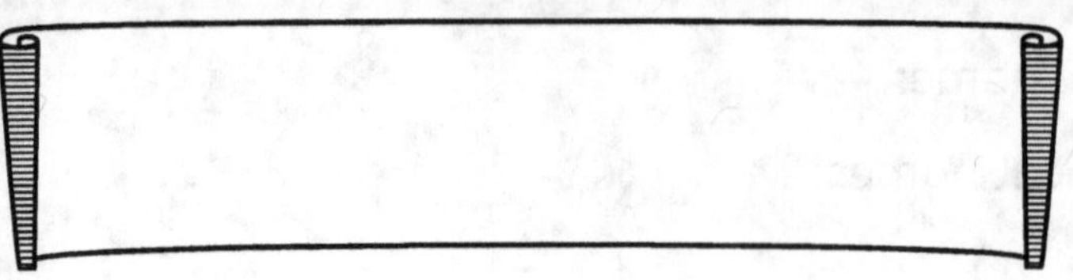

Scientific name:

Other local names:

Description:

Eating habits:

Habitat:

Web construction:

Other observations:

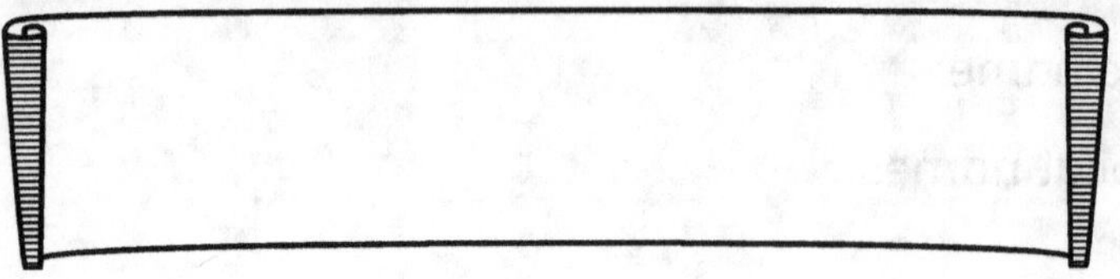

Scientific name:

Other local names:

Description:

Eating habits:

Habitat:

Web construction:

Other observations:

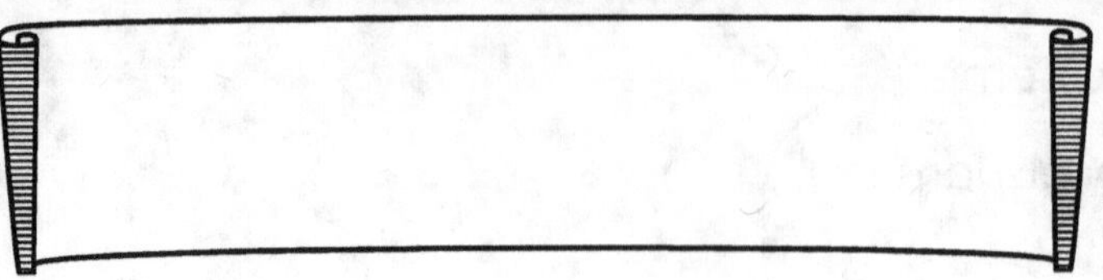

Scientific name:

Other local names:

Description:

Eating habits:

Habitat:

Web construction:

Other observations:

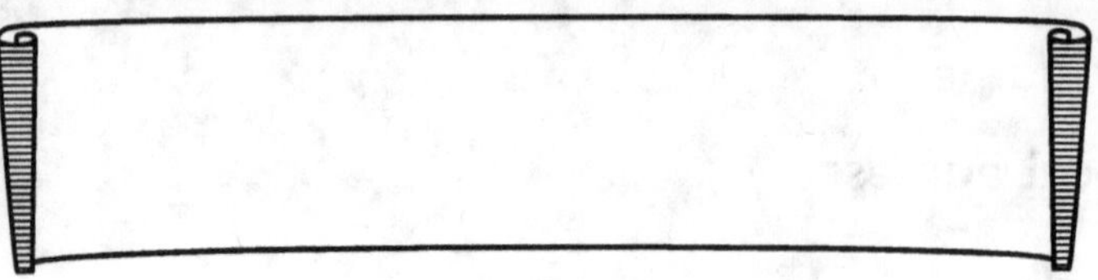

Scientific name:

Other local names:

Description:

Eating habits:

Habitat:

Web construction:

Other observations:

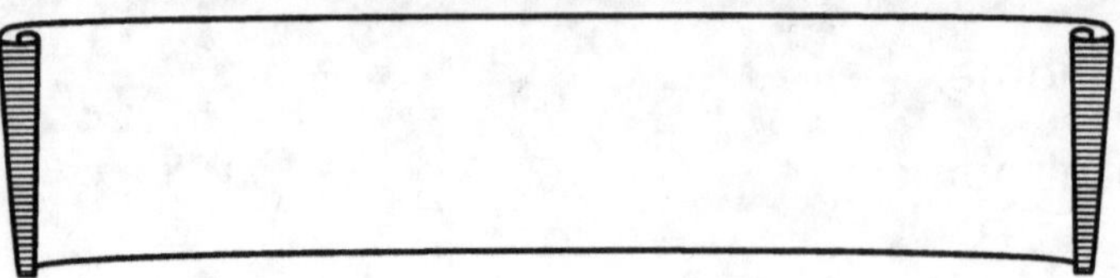

Scientific name:

Other local names:

Description:

Eating habits:

Habitat:

Web construction:

Other observations:

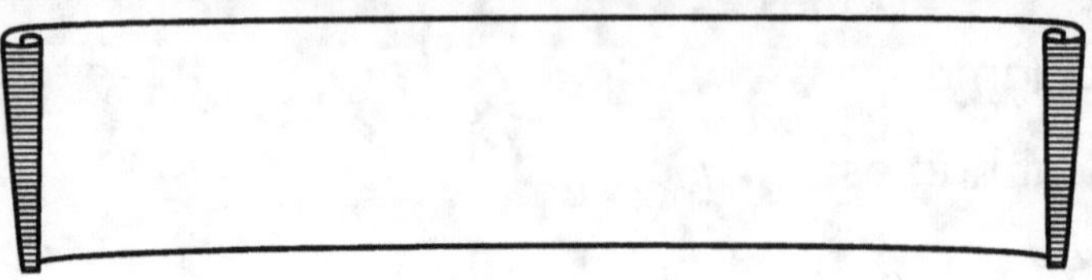

Scientific name:

Other local names:

Description:

Eating habits:

Habitat:

Web construction:

Other observations:

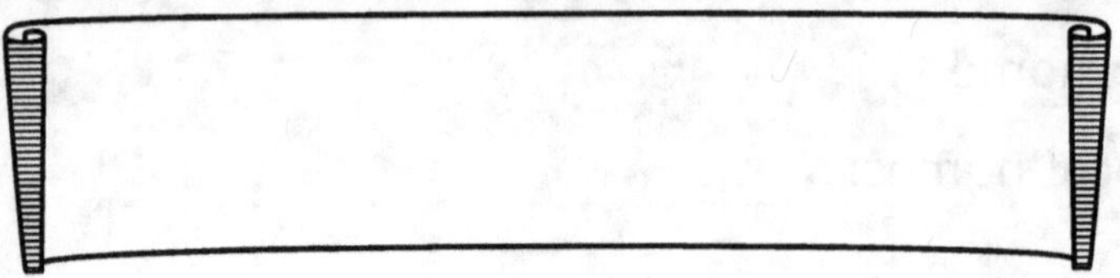

Scientific name:

Other local names:

Description:

Eating habits:

Habitat:

Web construction:

Other observations:

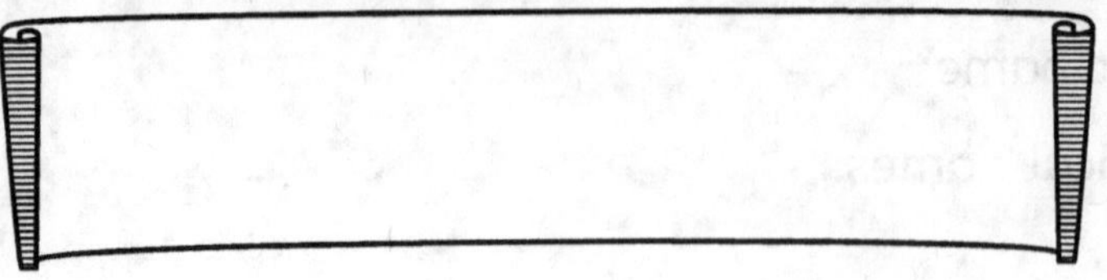

Scientific name:

Other local names:

Description:

Eating habits:

Habitat:

Web construction:

Other observations:

Did you Know?

There are approximately 40,000 known species of spiders in the world. There are no spiders in Antartica.

All spiders produce silk. They're used to make webs, and some spiders eat them as well.

All spiders produce venom. Not all of them are harmful to humans. And no, you don't turn into Spiderman.

A strand of spider silk is five times stronger than a strand of steel of the same thickness.

The "Goliath birdeater" is the largest spider in the world. The smallest spider in the world is "Patu digua".

The venom of a "Brown recluse spider" can damage skin tissue, cause fever, chills, rashes, blisters, and vomiting.

Spiders do not consume their prey. Chemicals are used to liquefy the body, which is then sucked up.

Bagheera Kiplingi, a jumping spider found in Central America, is the only known herbivorous spider.

There are about 30 spiders in the average home, and you are generally three feet away from one.

Spiders make silk with a variety of properties and thicknesses that are used for various tasks like drag lines, snares, web support, and egg cases.

Spiders have eight eyes, each with one lens. They are, however, all nearsighted.

Female spiders are known to have a voracious appetite and are known to lay up to 3,000 eggs at one time.

The "Sydney funnel-web spider" is known for its aggressive behaviour. When confronted, they will bite repeatedly rather than run away.

Spider silk is a liquid that solidifies when it is stretched after secretion.

Spider webs contain Vitamin K, a coagulant that can stop bleeding. They also have antiseptic and antifungal properties.

List of phone numbers

NAME

CONTACT NO.